UNLEASHED

CLARK CRAWFORD
FOREWORD BY ALLAN G. HEDBERG, Ph.D.

🏠 CrossHouse

Copyright by Clark Crawford, 2011
All Rights Reserved
Published by
CrossHouse Publishing,
2844 S. FM 549
Suite A
Rockwall, Texas 75032-9112
Printed in the United States of America
by Lightning Source, LaVergne, TN
Except where otherwise indicated, all Scripture taken from the Holy Bible,
New King James Version, copyright 1979 and 1980
by Thomas Nelson Publishers
Cover design by Dennis Davidson
Author photograph by Lindsay Grant, Life Essence Photography
lifeessencephotography.com

ISBN 978-1-61315-017-7
Library of Congress 2011940136

Dedication

This book is dedicated to my Lord, Savior, and best friend, Jesus Christ. He loved me when I was unlovable. He saved me when I did nothing to deserve it. He never leaves me nor forsakes me. I love Jesus more than life. I am determined to glorify Him and my Heavenly Father all the remaining days of my life.

This book is also dedicated to my two children, Conner Crawford and Kelsey Crawford. My life would not be the same without you in it. I am so thankful that you are my children. I love you both beyond words.

This book is also dedicated to the mother of our two children, Tamara Crawford. You have been faithful in raising our children through sickness and disease that almost took your life. You never once complained or wavered, even when you could or should have. You're a very special mother. I thank God that He chose you to be the mother of our children.

Finally this book is dedicated to all of the faithful ministers of the gospel of Jesus Christ. I thank you for your commitment to hurting people. Keep preaching the uncompromised Word of God. It never returns void.

Acknowledgements

As with any book, it takes a great team to pull all the elements together. I want to extend my personal thanks to:

Christopher R. Downs—Thank you for typing the manuscript and being so faithful to me and to Cross Times. You have gone above and beyond anything I could have ever expected. Your faithfulness to Jesus Christ and youth ministry is second to none.

Tracy Allen—Thank you for being my faithful friend for over 30 years now. Also, thank you for the title of this book, *Unleashed!* God seems to always use you with the titles of my books. You are a Godsend in my life.

Steve Rainey—I could not have asked for a more faithful board member and friend. Your wisdom and love for me is never taken for granted. You always have an on-time word. I love you Steve!

Louis Moore—CrossHouse Publishing. Thank you for being so good to me. You have always gone above and beyond my expectations regarding my books. Your character and integrity show without saying. I am so thankful to have you as a part of my life and ministry. Thank you for believing in me.

Table of Contents

Foreword	9
Introduction	11
Chapter 1 Pouring Out His Spirit	13
Chapter 2 Rivers of Living Water	19
Chapter 3 Clean Hands and a Pure Heart	23
Chapter 4 The Power of God	27
Chapter 5 The Fire of God	31
Chapter 6 All Things Are Possible	35
Chapter 7 It's Time to Get Right with God	39
Chapter 8 Love Defeats Every Enemy	43
Chapter 9 Dreamers	47
Chapter 10 The Kingdom of Heaven	51
Chapter 11 The Prize	55
Chapter 12 An Awakening	59
Chapter 13 Draw Near to God	63
Chapter 14 Last Day Anointing	67
Chapter 15 My Cup Runs Over	71
Chapter 16 Pain at The Cross	75
Chapter 17 The Blood Spill	79
Chapter 18 Crucified with Christ	83
Chapter 19 Unleashed	87
Appendix: The Sinner's Prayer	91
I Want To Hear From You	93
Clark's Other Books	95
Thoughts and Notes	97

Foreword

Unleashed is the fourth in a series of books written by Clark Crawford as he details the checkered and sordid history of his personal life. *Unleashed*, a sequel to his previous three books, outlines the theological basis for the miraculous changes he has experienced in his life and tells of the purpose for which he now lives. While Clark Crawford is neither a theological nor Bible scholar, he does understand the basic components of his living faith. His living faith is based on solid theological concepts drawn from the breath of scripture.

Unleashed is a basic manual of the essentials and fundamental tenets of the Christian faith. Every believer comes to a personal faith through an active process in search of God and Truth. It is the result of this search that the believer begins to understand and build a foundation of his or her personal faith that will mature and flourish. The basic tenets of the Christian faith as outlined by the author allow a new believer to become spiritually mature and intentional in living a Godly lifestyle.

Unleashed is essentially an outline of the pathway to maturity in faith. It is not just a book on the "basics of the faith for dummies", but the basics of the faith for all believers desiring to mature and understand the fundamental concepts and factors on which a living faith is grounded and daily life guided. Knowing God and experiencing His daily blessings is also a purpose of the book.

This book could be well used by a Sunday School class or a small-group Bible study to form the basis of an invigorating discussion on the essentials of the Christian faith. *Unleashed* is a giveaway book to help new believers know their Bible better.

Reading this book will not change your life, but it will provide the foundation stones for maturing your Christian faith.

Reading the book will not bring you to a faith in God, but it will give your faith in God perspective, understanding and a greater meaning.

Reading the book will not connect you with a fellowship of believers, but it will assist you in knowing how to seek out believers with whom to associate so that your faith will be developed and strengthened in a Godly manner.

This book will not be an easy read, but it will be an important read for the young and new believer.

Lastly, the book is not for the purpose of deciding if one should believe, but rather tells the story on what one's belief shall be based and substantiated.

I invite you to dig in and start the process of growing in faith.

> Allan G. Hedberg, Ph.D.
> Clinical Psychologist
> Fresno, California

Introduction

I have been waiting two years to write this book.

Two years ago when I began to write *Unleashed*, the Lord stopped me in my tracks while I was at a radio station and instructed me to write my last book, *Thank God for My Cross*. Now it is time for this book to be published. I believe God Himself is going to use this book to unleash the Third Great Awakening to the world. God is about to pour out His Spirit on all flesh and no man will be able to deny that God has done this.

I believe this spiritual awakening will be like no other. God always saves the best for last. He says the latter will be greater than the former.

My prayer is that all people will come to their wits end as God sends down the latter rain. I believe that we will see men, women, and children falling on their faces before a Holy God, repenting, and turning from their wicked ways.

I see multitudes running to the cross and crying out, "God have mercy on me a sinner." I see the blood of Jesus washing their sins away into the sea of forgetfulness. I see families being restored. I see marriages being restored. I see addicts instantly being set free. I see signs and wonders possessing the land. I see lonely people in the arms of a loving God. I see people who were once abused being loved and used of God. I see children no longer being abused or molested. I see murderers repenting the same way Paul did and then impacting their world for Jesus Christ.

I see the last first and the first last.

I see liars and cheaters on their faces at the cross weeping and surrendering their lives to Christ. I see the weak strong and the prideful humbled.

Friends, I believe that through this book, you will be encouraged to let God use your life to flow His power and might through you. God wants to unleash Himself by His Spirit in the earth and has chosen you as the temple of His dwelling.

Do you see the Third Great Awakening coming? Can you hear the rattling of angels wings getting prepared for war? As the wind blows without you seeing it, so does the Spirit of God hover over the earth, waiting for Almighty God to say, "Go ye into all the world and preach the gospel to every creature."

The greatest day and hour are upon us. Don't be one who doubts the coming of our great and mighty King.

Yield to God as you read this book cover to cover. It might just be that as His Spirit is unleashed into our world, you're the one that God wants to use during the Third Great Awakening. God's desire is to bring heaven to earth.

Now is the time! Enjoy your journey through this book. You will never be the same!

Chapter 1

Pouring Out His Spirit

And it shall come to pass afterward that I will pour out My Spirit on all flesh; your sons and your daughters shall prophecy, your old men shall dream dreams, your young men shall see visions. And also on My menservants and on My maidservants I will pour out My Spirit in those days (Joel 2:28-29).

God is about to unleash His Spirit into the earth like no man or woman has ever before seen. The Third Great Awakening is going to change our world very soon. Many will see it and fear. Through it many others will begin to trust in the Lord.

Sadly but true, a disaster is often needed for people to fall on their knees, repent, and cry out to God. This repentance and turn to God will not be a disaster, though the events leading up to it may seem to many people like one. During this time I believe more people than ever in history will be saved. I believe that the Lord is going to show Himself to humankind in a way that causes people to fall in love with Him. When God's Spirit falls down, it will bring conviction of sin, righteousness, and judgment. His Spirit will expose to a hurting generation the wickedness of man's heart.

Friends, we are in need of a revival. People are dying and going to hell everyday. People are committing suicide at an all-time high. Mothers and fathers are murdering their children in record numbers. Today more than ever before young women are having abortions. The divorce rate is higher than ever. More than ever children are being molested and abused. We have more drug addicts, alcoholics, gamble-holics, pornography addicts and perversion than ever in history.

We need God to pour out His Spirit on us more today than in any other generation.

The devil has come to steal, kill, and destroy. He knows that his time is short. He is intent on taking as many as he can to his final destination—hell! He is going to burn in a lake of fire forever. The Bible points out the sad truth that the road to hell is broad and many easily find it. The road to heaven is narrow and few find it.

I am determined to take as many to heaven with me as I can—through the power and Spirit of the Living God. I want to encourage every person who is reading this book, to re-evaluate his or her walk in life. Are you really saved and going to heaven? Or are you one who thinks you are, but you're really going to be in for a rude awakening when Jesus suddenly shows up?

Before I go further in this book, I want to make sure that everyone of my readers knows Jesus Christ as his or her personal Savior and Lord. I know many readers are Christians, but like Jesus I need to be sure about the one sheep who may not truly be in the flock of Christ.

Here is a scripture that I want you to ponder in your heart:

"Not everyone who says to me 'Lord, Lord," shall enter the Kingdom of heaven, but he who does the will of My Father in heaven. Many will say to Me in that day, 'Lord, Lord, have we not prophesied in Your name, cast out demons in Your name, and done many wonders in your name?' And then I will declare to them, 'I never knew you; depart from me, you who practice lawlessness," (Matthew 7:21-23).

Because of their good works, many people think they are saved, but they are in for a shock when they stand before Jesus Christ at His judgment seat. Do not let this be you. I want to encourage you this very moment to pray this simple prayer out loud and mean it to the best of your ability.

Say, "Dear Jesus, I repent of all my sins. I admit I am a sinner. I need Your grace and You. Wash me in the blood and give me a new life. I confess you as my Lord and Savior. I believe in my heart that God raised You from the dead. In Jesus name I pray, Amen."

If you just prayed that prayer and believed it in your heart, then you are saved. Congratulations! Because of your decision, the angels are throwing a big party in heaven this very moment. The Bible says that Jesus leaves the 99 to go after that one lost person. You are on His heart. He has been so good to you and me.

Now, His Spirit will begin to work in you and change everything about you. You are so loved today.

I praise God that he poured out His Spirit on you today. You're a new creation. As the Bible says, old things are now passed away; everything becomes new for you from this moment on.

It does not even matter what you did before this moment in time. Your past is washed away by the blood and death of Jesus Christ on that old rugged cross at Calvary. Never look back, except when you give your testimony one day. A testimony is to let people know who you were before Jesus came into your heart and saved you. After you tell people who you were before you became a Christian—whether you were an alcoholic, a drug addict, a liar, a thief, an abuser, an adulterer or a sexually immoral person—tell them what He did for you today. God gets all the glory for how He had mercy on you throughout all the days of sin. You could have died and gone to hell. You could be sick today, if not for the grace of God. You could have contracted AIDS or some other disease, if not for the grace of God.

Now go tell everyone how faithful God is and that He will do for others what He has done for you.

God is no respecter of persons. He is not willing that any should perish, but that everyone would come to the knowledge of Jesus Christ—just like you did today. Praise God!

Now you need to get into a Bible-teaching church. Get around the right people. The Bible says bad company corrupts good morals. Read the Bible and pray every day in Jesus' name. The Holy Spirit will lead you and guide you all the days of your life.

Thank God for pouring out His Spirit on you and others today.

The Bible says that no man comes to the Father, unless the Spirit draws him. That is why we need God to pour out His Spirit on all flesh in these last days. Man cannot change a heart. Only God by His Spirit can change a life. We do our part by telling people the Word of God and loving them, but the Holy Spirit does the work.

You are now the hands and feet of Jesus. As you grow in Christ, you will learn to love, forgive, and have compassion for all people, even your enemies. You will learn more about that later in this book. You are now the answer to someone's prayer. Today, you are someone's miracle. I want to encourage you to tell someone you got saved today. Jesus died publicly for you and He wants you to publicly tell someone what He has done this day for you. Let your light shine, my friend, because you are going places you never dreamed possible.

Prayer:

Dear Jesus, thank you for saving me today. Thank you for pouring out Your Spirit on me this day. In Jesus name I pray, Amen.

Scripture to meditate on:

For God so loved the world that He gave His only begotten Son, that whoever believes in Him should not perish but have everlasting life (John 3:16).

Chapter 2

Rivers of Living Water

On the last day, that great day of the feast, Jesus stood and cried out, saying, "If anyone thirsts, let him come to me and drink. He who believes in Me, as the scripture has said, out of his heart will flow rivers of living water" (John 7:37-39).

The Third Great Awakening is about to come to the world.

It is time to start praying and calling out to God for mercy. Every place this living water touches will bring life. Friends, dead and dry things will begin to live again. This may be you or your family members. Living water from heaven brings life to the dead and dry.

Remember what God spoke to Ezekiel in his 37th chapter regarding the dry bones?

"The hand of the Lord came upon me and brought me out in the Spirit of the Lord, and set me down in the midst of the valley; and it was full of bones. Then He caused me to pass by them all around, and behold, there were very many in the open valley; and indeed they were very dry. And He said to me 'Son of man, can these bones live?' So I answered, 'O Lord God, you know.'

"Again He said to me, "Prophecy to these bones, and say to them, 'O dry bones, hear the word of the Lord! Thus says the Lord God to these bones: surely I will cause breath to enter

into you, and you shall live. I will put sinews on you and bring flesh upon you, cover you with skin and put breath in you; and you shall live. Then you shall know that I am the Lord."

"So I prophesied as I was commanded, and as I prophesied, there was a noise, and suddenly a rattling; and the bones came together, bone to bone. Indeed, as I looked, the sinews and the flesh came upon them, and the skin covered them over; but there was no breath in them. Also He said to me, "Prophesy to the breath, prophesy, son of man, and say to the breath, "Thus says the Lord God: Come from the four winds, O breath, and breathe on these slain that they may live." So I prophesied as he commanded me, and breath came into them, and they lived, and stood upon their feet, an exceedingly great army," (Ezekiel 37:1-10).

Can you hear the Lord speaking to you through these scriptures? Friends, this is a sign of what is about to happen, as God unleashes His Spirit to bring about the Third Great Awakening.

Hear me, it will be here before you know it; you must prepare yourselves—or you will be consumed by fear and could become shipwrecked.

Open your spiritual eyes and ears. As you see the trees move by the wind, so shall the spiritual see His Spirit blow in an awakening that is going to shake the very foundation of this earth.

Drunkards, sexually immoral people, drug addicts—all those in the wrong place at the wrong time—will be consumed and never heard from again. It will be too late for them in the same way it was too late for those who had no oil left in their lamps.

The Bible says Jesus is going to return like a thief in the night, without any warning and without any precise time or date on your schedule He will be here. Now is the time to choose life, not death. Many think they will have the opportunity to repent before they die, but remember that you could die in your sleep tonight. You could suddenly end up in a head-on car collision. Your heart beat could stop at any moment. You never know when your time will be up. Hear me clearly: you are going to die! Where will you spend eternity? Are you leaving a legacy for your children and others? Are you a stumbling block for others? Or are you glorifying your Father in heaven?

Believe it or not, we are in the greatest days to be alive—that is if you know Christ as your personal Lord and Savior. Now if you are not a child of God, then you are in for the worst days of your life. Like no other time fear is gripping people in the world today. Apart from Christ fear breeds on every side. People are losing their homes at an all-time high. People are going bankrupt in unprecedented numbers. People are suppressing their fear, pain and suffering with drugs, alcohol, pornography, gambling, prostitution, hate, unforgiveness, other forms of sexual immorality, and bitterness. They are dying on the inside. Sickness and disease are overtaking many today as well.

We need an awakening of God's love and power to hit our homes, churches, and work places soon. Only prayer and repentance will change America. My prayer is that as God's Spirit is unleashed people from all walks of life will fall on their knees and repent of their wickedness. When they give their lives to Jesus Christ, they will live again.

People are dry everywhere you go. We need to speak to the dry bones the same way that Ezekiel did. God wants to give to the hopeless life and life more abundantly. He is not willing that any should perish but that everyone would be saved. That is why he continues to have mercy on the sinner. But He makes it very clear that He will not always strive with man. The day will arrive when He says enough is enough! That is when it is too late for that person and judgment consumes him or her.

Take this as a warning. Ask the Lord to help you right now. Do not harden your heart. This could be your last chance. It is no accident that you are reading this book at this very moment. God has your number; this is your day to choose life. Let the tears flow. Right now let the brokenness take you into the arms of a loving God, who chased you down to this very place in time. I am asking you to pray this prayer right now— and mean it to the best of your ability. God has a plan for your life that is so awesome, that everyone, including even you, will say, "Only God could have done this!"

Prayer:

Dear Jesus, thank you for rescuing me today. Thank you for dying on the cross for me. I repent of my sins. I ask you to wash me in your blood. Save me Jesus. Give me a new life. In Jesus' name I pray, Amen.

Scripture to meditate on:

"For I know the thoughts that I think towards you," says the Lord, "thoughts of peace and not of evil, to give you a future and a hope" (Jeremiah 29:11).

Chapter 3

Clean Hands and a Pure Heart

Who may ascend into the hill of the Lord? Or who may stand in His holy place? He who has clean hands and a pure heart. Who has not lifted up his soul to an idol nor sworn deceitfully (Psalm 24:3-4).

If you want to be someone the Lord uses to unleash His power and Spirit through, then you must have clean hands and a pure heart. God is holy, so you must remain pure and clean in order for Him to use you. This does not mean you will not blow it every once in a while. Only Jesus was perfect. But He does require you to quickly repent and return to Him, so He can count on you. Your body is His temple and this next scripture tells you what to do.

"Or do you not know that your body is the temple of the Holy Spirit who is in you, whom you have from God, and you are not your own? For you were bought at a price, therefore glorify God in your body and in your spirit, which are God's," (1 Corinthians 6:19-20).

Is it very important to pray and spend quality time with God. Every day you are the answer to someone's prayer. You are someone's miracle. There is someone God is putting in your path each day who needs an encouraging word. When you have clean hands and a pure heart, you can hear God more clearly. You will be more concerned with others than you are with yourself. I have found that when I am helping others out of their messes, then God takes good care of mine.

When you seek first the Kingdom of God and His righteousness, He adds everything you need. God is more than enough. His eyes are running to and fro throughout the whole earth, to show Himself strong on behalf of those whose heart is loyal toward Him.

If you delight yourself in the Lord, then He will give you the desires of your heart.

The Bible says that there is a way that seems right to a man, but the end is death. God's ways are higher than our ways, and His thoughts are higher than our thoughts. He always knows what is best for you. He sees the end from the beginning. People get in real trouble when they fall into sin. It blinds them. Sin hardens your heart. The little foxes spoil the vine. It starts off with a little lie, or just one glass of wine. But many times it turns to major stuff.

The devil is a liar and deceiver.

He makes sin seem pleasurable at the moment, and for a while it is. But sin always brings forth death. You will always reap what you sow. If you sow to the flesh, you will of the flesh reap corruption. If you live with someone outside of marriage, you are heading for disaster. If you have sex outside of marriage, you are doomed for destruction. I know! I have been there, done that, and have the t-shirt. Ha! Really, it is not funny at all. If you will listen to someone who has been down that road, you will save yourself a lot of heartache and trouble.

The Bible says there is nothing hidden that will not be brought to light. Your sin will find you out. All you have to do is ask some of the movie stars and professional athletes. I am not going to say names in this book, but many have been exposed publicly. We are seeing them on the news even now, going through divorces; their children are suffering for their selfishness.

I have a saying, you can either humble yourself in secret with God and make things right, or He will humble you publicly. I know about that too!

There is a saying, "You don't know what you've got until it is gone." Don't find out the hard way like I did. Job lost everything in the blink of an eye. Clark did too! I never thought it would happen to me. Many of you feel the same way.

I want to encourage every husband to love his wife and children. They can be gone just like that. Don't think for a second that it cannot happen to you. When you found your wife, you found a good thing and obtained favor from the Lord. It may just be that the mercy God has shown you is because of your wife. Get into church and serve God and people. He wants to give you clean hands and a pure heart. You can love if you will allow God to fill you. You can stop abusing the people you love the most. You can stop drinking, drugging, the pornography, gambling and other things that have you bound.

It is not too late for your marriage or relationship with your children. It is not too late to make amends with that person who abused you, or with the people you abused. God is a God of second, third, fourth, fifth, sixth, etc., chances. It is never too late.

It starts with turning to Jesus and repenting of your sins. The moment you repent and ask Him to save you, forgive you, and restore you, is the moment your life changes forever.

Do it! Your future and family depend on it. More than that, heaven or hell awaits your decision.

Prayer:

Dear Jesus, I ask you to give me clean hands and a pure heart. I turn my life and future over to you right now. I surrender to your will and way. In Jesus name I pray, Amen.

Scripture to meditate on:

Create in me a clean heart O God, and renew a steadfast spirit within me. Do not cast me away from your presence, and do not take Your Holy Spirit from me (Psalm 51:10-11).

Chapter 4

The Power of God

And I, brethren, when I came to you, did not come with excellence of speech or of wisdom declaring to you the testimony of God. For I am determined not to know anything among you except Jesus Christ and Him crucified. I was with you in weakness, in fear, and in much trembling. And my speech and my preaching were not with persuasive words of human wisdom but in demonstration of the Spirit and of power, that your faith should not be in the wisdom of men, but in the power of God (1 Corinthians 2:1-5).

The power of God is about to be unleashed from heaven to earth. This power will bring about a spiritual awakening to the lost and hurting people of today.

The Bible says it is not by man's might or man's power, but by My Spirit, says the Lord of hosts.

God wants to demonstrate His power on the earth today. It is His will that heaven come to earth. Listen to the Lord's prayer.

Our Father, which art in heaven, hallowed be Thy name. Thy kingdom come, Thy will be done, on earth as it is in heaven . . .. God is about to unleash heaven to earth. He is going to do it through people as well as ways beyond our comprehension. You may have an angel wake you up one night, or come knocking on your door. The Bible even says do not forget to entertain strangers, for by doing so some have unwittingly entertained angels (Hebrews 13:2). I believe that we are going to see things we previously have never seen. I believe we are going to do things we have never done. I believe we are going to hear things we have never heard. I believe we will speak things we have never spoken.

Friends, if you are saved, then you have living inside you the same Spirit and power that raised Jesus from the dead. The same power that parted the Red Sea lives in you. The same power that caused a shepherd boy to defeat a giant is on the inside of you. The same power that was in the fiery furnace with Shadrach, Meshach and Abednego is with you. The same power that was in the lion's den with Daniel indwells in you. The same power that blinded and transformed Paul on the road to Damascus as well as the same power that caused Lazarus and Jairus' daughter to be raised from the dead is in you, too.

Yes friends, God is the same yesterday, today and forever. You are going to see the full gospel lived out in these last days. Don't be surprised when God uses you to raise the dead or see cancer fall off bodies. Don't be surprised when you walk in a room and people begin to fall on their knees repenting and crying out to God because His glory is being unleashed through you. You're His temple and dwelling place. Expect His power to produce miracles, signs, wonders, salvations, healings, and other supernatural happenings everywhere you go.

And please keep in mind, where God moves in a mighty way, there always will be religious people that rise up against you and the work you are doing. It happened to Jesus and it will happen to you. But rejoice when this happens because the Bible says blessed is he who is persecuted for the sake of righteousness, for great is his reward in heaven.

Stand on this next scripture at all times.

"Behold, I give you the authority to trample on serpents

and scorpions, and over all the power of the enemy, and nothing shall by any means hurt you," (Luke 10:19).

No weapon formed against you shall prosper. If God is for you, then who can be against you? God has proven Himself time and time again to me that this scripture is true. He is a strong tower and a mighty fortress. He delivers out of the hand of the enemy time after time again. If that were not so, you would have been swallowed up long ago. Believe me, the devil hates you and wants you dead and in hell with him. He hates your family, children, and everything good. If you give him an inch, he will take a mile. Again, he wants you dead. If not for God's grace on your life, you would be dead, sick, or in hell for eternity.

My prayer for you who are reading this book is that you would first and foremost make everything right with God and His Son Jesus Christ at this very moment. You and I cannot afford to live a moment outside the protection of God.

For God so loved you that He gave His only begotten Son, Jesus, to be murdered, so that you could be saved and spend eternity with Him.

He is faithful. He is a rewarder of those who diligently seek Him. He is watching over His Word to perform it in your life. Your greatest days are just ahead. Your latter days will be greater than your former.

With God all things are possible. All you have to do is believe by faith that God can do what He has promised you and me through the Word of God. The Bible is the gospel. Gospel means good news. I love reading and living out the Word of God. Paul said he was the written epistle. People are watching you and me everywhere we go. We are either glorifying God or the devil. We are either walking by faith or fear. We either love or hate. We either have peace or no rest at all. There will never be another day like today.

As you read this book I want to encourage you to love your

husband or wife and children . You never know if this will be their last day alive—or even your last day on this earth. Live every day like it is your last. You do not want to have any regrets. People are on medicine, drugs, and alcohol today because of guilt, shame and unforgiveness. They would tell you right now if they could, that if they had it all to do over again, they would have lived differently. But the truth is, you have only one chance. Now, go hug your wife or husband and children. Tell them how thankful you are to have them in your life. Now, call that person that you have never forgiven. You do not want to go to your grave with unforgiveness in your heart.

Listen, God's power will enable you to do anything you want to do—or dare to dream to do. This is your day to shine!

Prayer:

Dear Jesus, I ask you to give me the power to do what I have never done. Give me the power to love and forgive. Thank you Jesus for answering my prayer. Amen.

Scripture to meditate on:

For the message of the cross is foolishness to those who are perishing, but to us who are being saved it is the power of God (1 Corinthians 1:18).

Chapter 5

The Fire of God

Therefore, since we are receiving a Kingdom which cannot be shaken, let us have grace, by which we may serve God acceptably with reverence and Godly fear. For our God is a consuming fire (Hebrews 12:28-29).

Friends, when God unleashes His fire it consumes all things that are impure and unholy. This should put a Godly fear in everyone reading this book.

It is time to get right with God, or you could be consumed by this fire.

Listen to what Jeremiah said: *Circumcise yourselves to the Lord, and take away the foreskins of your hearts, you men of Judah and inhabitants of Jerusalem, lest my fury come forth like fire and burn so that no one can quench it, because of the evil you are doing* (Jeremiah 4:4).

The Bible also says it is a fearful thing to fall into the hands of the living God (Hebrews 10:31). God is serious when He says to be holy as He is holy.

It is amazing to me how people always run to a fire. Whether it is a house, building, or apartment complex, they will follow the smoke to a fire.

This fire of God is going to spread like wildfire. I hear the Lord saying that there will be places of revival fires, where people will go to experience the presence of God like never before. Make sure your heart is right when you approach this all-consuming fire. It surely will burn up the things that cannot remain.

Gold is purified by fire. You are gold in God's eyes. Jeremiah said that the Word of God was like fire shut up in his bones. He could not contain it.

This is the same way the fire burns in my heart. Everywhere I go, the Spirit of God unleashes His Word through me. I literally cannot contain it. People at work call me "Man on Fire!" What a compliment of God's great grace. He wants to set you and me on fire and bring people to watch us burn for Jesus.

I believe that His fire is the glory of God.

Listen to this scripture: *Arise, shine; For your light has come! And the glory of the Lord is risen upon you* (Isaiah 60:1).

The glory of God resting on you is His fire. People will be drawn to the fire and glory on your life. Get ready to be unleashed at your work place, church, restaurants, etc. People are going to start coming up to you for what seems like no reason at all. Remember, no man comes to the Father except that the Spirit of God draws him. As God burns this fire in and upon you, people will come. Be ready in season and out of season.

You are His hands and His feet. You are His voice on the earth. He is coming to unleash the Third Great Awakening. Will you be ready? Will you allow Him to set you on fire, so that as people come to you and you are able to speak the uncompromised Word of God? Can you be trusted? It is time to let the fire of God's Word purge you, prove you, and burn away every unrighteous thing in you and in your life.

Remember, God is an all-consuming fire. His fire wants to be shut up in your bones to where you cannot contain it. Read the Word daily; pray the Word daily. Get so full of the Word that it is unleashed through you without you having to do anything but be that vessel through which He flows.

Do you remember the story in Daniel chapter 3 about the three Hebrew children? They would not bow down to Nebuchadnezzar's golden image. So they were cast into the burning fiery furnace. The king set the furnace seven times hotter than before. The only people consumed were the guards who cast them in. The Hebrew children came out unburned without even a smell of smoke on them.

Listen, if you are holy as He is holy, then Jesus is with you in the fire. But if you are living in willful sin, living a godless life, then this very moment you should be experiencing a fear of God because of what you just read. The guards were consumed in this fire, and you will be too, unless you repent and turn from your wicked ways. At the end of this chapter you will have another opportunity to accept Jesus as Lord and Savior. You can have a new life and not have to fear death ever again.

Listen to this scripture: *Behold, I have refined you, but not as silver, I have tested you in the furnace of affliction* (Isaiah 48:10).

Are you suffering today? Let me tell you first hand, this is one of the many ways God refines you. Jesus even learned obedience by the things which He suffered. My greatest lessons and growth came from intense suffering. Whether it be prison, jail, abuse, alcoholism, drug addiction, etc. This is what refined me in the fire and brought me forth as pure gold. I am more dependent on Jesus and my heavenly Father today than I have ever been. He taught me so many things through my suffering and pain. Without Him I can do nothing. What you start in the flesh you have to finish in the flesh. No fun at all.

I also learned that the flesh profits you nothing. It is when we are weak that we are really strong. When we humble ourselves and allow God to do what He wants with us, God steps in and says "Now I can use you."

Will you surrender your life today? The fire of God is coming to earth. As a matter of fact, many are on fire today for Jesus. But God is about to unleash a fire seven times more evident than anything we have seen in this generation. You do not want to be caught slumbering and in willful sin. You could be one of those consumed as the fire of God spreads from city to city, state to state, country to country, and nation to nation.

I feel it getting a little hotter as I end this chapter.

Prayer:

Dear Jesus, I repent of my sins the best that I know how. Please forgive me and wash me in the blood. I ask You to set me on fire and bring people to watch me burn for You as You refine me in Your fire. In Jesus name I pray, Amen.

Scripture to meditate on:

It is a fearful thing to fall into the hands of the living God (Hebrews 10:31).

Chapter 6

All Things Are Possible

But Jesus looked at them and said, "With men it is impossible, but not with God; for with God all things are possible" (Mark 10:27).

The chief sin of the Israelites in Psalm 78:41 was that they limited the Holy One of Israel. I also believe this is the chief sin of people today. If we really believe that all things are possible with God, then we would not be in the predicaments we find ourselves in today.

The truth is, there is nothing too difficult for God. He created heaven, earth, the seas, and everything in them. If you read the book of Jonah, you will see that God was in control of the ship, the people on the ship, the wind, and the storm, the great fish, the plant, the worm, and even Jonah. God controls all of nature and everything within it. Yes, you have your own will, but friends, regardless of what people tell you, it is a limited will. The devil cannot do anything to you unless he gets permission from God first.

All you have to do is look at the stories of Job and Peter. Satan had to ask God to sift Peter as wheat (Luke 22:31). Satan could only do to Job what God allowed him to do. All you have to do is read Job chapter 1 and 2.

If God allows something in your life, then you can rest assured that He has a plan and purpose for it.

What about Joseph? His brothers sold him into slavery and he ended up in a prison. Yet one night he went to bed a prisoner and woke up the next day the prime minister of an entire nation. Within 24 hours his life changed forever.

What the devil meant for evil God turned for good in the lives of these great men of faith.

Friends, all things (good, bad, and ugly) really do work together for good. When you realize this fact—as well as that God is in control of all things—then your life will never be the same. If God was not in control of your life and mine, then I can assure you that you would be dead and in hell. The devil has meant to steal, kill and destroy you and me. If it was not for the grace and mercy of God, he would have done these things when we were lost and in sin. God in His everlasting love and mercy protected you all those years of drinking, drugging, sexual immorality, jealousy, rage, hatred, unforgiveness, adultery, suicide attempts, prostitution and abortions.

God is good. You need to begin to praise Him and thank Him right now for making a way for you when there seemed to be no way. His hand has always been on you, but now is the time to surrender your life totally to Him. He is the One who has never left you nor forsaken you. He is the One who has never abused you. He is the one who has loved you unconditionally—when nobody else did. He is the One who hung on a cross and had nails driven through His hands and feet for you and me. He is the One that had a crown of thorns gashed into His head. He is the One who took 39 stripes upon His back as flesh and blood fell from His body. He is the One who said regarding you and me, "Father, forgive them, for they do not know what they are doing."

I don't know anyone else that would do all this for me. Do you? I don't think so either! All things are possible to him who believes. Yes, God raised Jesus from the dead. It seems impossible, but oh how true it is. Scientists and others have tried to prove this wrong, but they admit that Jesus is alive and He was raised from the dead. Period!

And today God wants to demonstrate His Spirit and power in your life the same way. If you are lost or backslidden, then today God wants to raise you spiritually from the dead. You can be born again spiritually this very moment. If you are not saved, then you are a dead man walking. If you don't give your life to Christ, you one day will die lost. That means you will die, then stand before the judgment seat of Christ one day, and He will say to you, "Depart from me you worker of lawlessness for I never knew you."

You will then be cast into hell and burn forever and ever. Throughout eternity you will be separated from a loving God. They say the worst part of hell is knowing that Jesus gave you an opportunity to have a relationship with Him, yet you rejected Him and said no. Wouldn't it be very sad one day to end up in hell while all your family is in heaven? Then on the other side of the coin, wouldn't it be sad to end up in heaven and have all of your family be in hell?

Here is the point. Give your life to Jesus Christ, then go win your family and friends to Christ. I don't want any of my family, friends, or anyone else going to hell. That is why I preach the gospel everywhere I can. Whether it be through books, churches, radio, television, prisons, jails, restaurants, Facebook, etc., I am determined to fill heaven with humanity and defeat the works of darkness—as God unleashes His Spirit and power through this vessel.

You are the answer to someone who has been praying for years. You are someone's miracle today and every day. You are the answer to someone about to commit suicide. You are the answer to someone who is about to overdose. You are the answer to a young single girl about to have an abortion. You are the answer to someone who is about to molest a child.

Now get right with God and let Him unleash you into peoples' lives so others will not be innocent victims of Satan's snares.

Prayer:

Dear Jesus, I repent of all my sins. I repent for limiting You. I believe that with You all things are possible. Wash me in Your blood and use me to unleash Your Spirit and power into my generation and those You want to save through my life. In Jesus name I pray. Amen.

Scripture to meditate on:

Now to Him who is able to do exceedingly abundantly above all that we ask or think, according to the power that works in us (Ephesians 3:20).

Chapter 7
It's Time To Get Right With God

Behold, now is the accepted time; behold, now is the day of salvation (2 Corinthians 6:2).

This chapter is for all who have backslidden from the Lord. Backsliding is a biblical term that means "falling away, turning away, apostasy." According to the apostle Paul, who wrote the verse above, *"Today is the day of mercy and grace."* In other words, if you ever plan to believe, that time is now.

Friends, this statement by Paul is both an invitation and a warning. The warning is as follows: Do not receive the grace of God in vain. Do not ignore, neglect or cast aside God's offer of mercy. Respond to it today, or you may never have another chance. Psalm 103:9 says, *"He will not always strive with us, nor will He keep His anger forever."*

Jesus warned that many believers would turn away and grow cold: *"Because iniquity shall abound, the love of many shall wax cold"* (Matthew 24:12). His message is clear: Many who have been on fire for the things of God are going to fall away.

Friends, it is time to fall at the foot of the cross and repent of coldness of heart. We are in the last days and you must not just go to the cross, but you must die there and let Jesus resurrect His life in you. All of the backsliding we see today—the turning away from faith to unbelief—comes at a time when you would least expect it. Rather, you would expect people to be drawing nearer to God. We are at the beginning of those days of "great sorrows" that Jesus referred to.

Even prominent voices in the world today agree: These are days of unspeakable wickedness, marked by uncontrollable greed, rampant sexual perversions, and multitudes giving themselves over to addictions of all kinds, from drugs to alcohol to pornography. Some who have backslidden tell themselves, "I can get right with the Lord any time I choose. I'm just not ready. I'm not mad at God; I just need time with my friends and time to enjoy myself. I know God is loving and merciful. When I'm ready, I'll come to Him. I'll know when that time is right." I hear these thoughts especially from the young people today. But remember what God said in Psalm 103:9. He will not always strive with you nor keep His anger forever. Is it really worth taking the chance? I don't think so! The Holy Spirit has compelled me to show you the danger of coldness. It is not that God turns aside from those who backslide; his grace is offered continuously. The blood of Christ toward sinners will never lose its power. But coldness has a powerful and predictable effect. Remember friends, I know because I lived through it to tell you these truths. You do not have to go through it if you will just hear the spirit of the Lord and obey.

The term "hardness" indicates a condition that is beyond the influence of any gracious pleadings, any persuading from the Holy Spirit. It begins with coldness—a self-imposed exclusion from God, with no intention of obeying the call of His gospel. For those who continue in coldness to God's voice—who keep distant from the Holy Spirit—hardness is the result. Hebrews offers this warning: *"Take heed, brethren, lest there be in any of you an evil heart of unbelief in departing from the living God. But exhort one another daily, while it is called today lest any of you be hardened through the deceitfulness of sin"* (Heb. 3:12-13).

Dear one, I exhort you right now, as Hebrews instructs, wherefore as the Holy Ghost saith, Today if ye will hear His voice, harden not your hearts, as (Israel did), in the day of temptation in the wilderness (Hebrews 3:7, 8). *"Let us hold fast our profession of faith"* (Heb. 4:14). God help us in these uncertain days to "take heed," lest any of us become hardened in heart in the day of our trial! You may think you could never harden your heart. But difficult times and trials are guaranteed to come to all who follow Jesus; no one is exempt. Therefore, *"Today, if you will hear His voice, do not harden your hearts"* (Heb. 4:7).

Prayer:

Father, open my eyes and heart to your truths and promises. Please don't allow me to harden my heart or become cold toward you. I repent of all sin and backsliding. In Jesus name. Amen!

Scripture To Meditate On:

But know this, that if the master of the house had known what hour the thief would come, he would have watched and not allowed his house to be broken into. Therefore you also be ready, for the Son of Man is coming at an hour you do not expect (Luke 12:39, 40).

Watch therefore, for you know neither the day nor the hour in which the Son of Man is coming (Matthew 25:13).

Preach the Word! Be ready in season and out of season. Convince, rebuke, exhort with all long suffering and teaching. For the time will come when they will not endure sound doctrine, but according to their own desires, because they have itching ears, they will heap up for themselves teachers, and they will turn their ears away from the truth and be turned aside to fables. But you be watchful in all things, endure afflictions, do the work of an evangelist, fulfill your ministry (2 Timothy 4:2-5).

Chapter 8

Love Defeats Every Enemy

For I am persuaded that neither death nor life, nor angels nor principalities nor powers, nor things present nor things to come, nor height nor depth, nor any other created thing, shall be able to separate us from the love of God which is in Christ Jesus our Lord (Romans 8:38-39).

When I first became aware of the fact that I had an enemy, Satan, who wanted to kill, steal, and destroy everything good God had planned for me, I was very interested in learning how to defeat him. While studying I learned many interesting biblical principles. I began attempting to exercise my authority as a believer. I rebuked evil spirits, cast them out, bound them, and loosed the Spirit of God. I fasted, resisted, stood firm, and made some progress, but I was not walking in the power that I am today. Something was missing. I was starving to live in the reality of the scriptures like these spoken by Jesus to his disciples:

"I will give you the keys of the kingdom of heaven, and whatever you bind on earth will be bound in heaven, and whatever you loose on earth will be loosed in heaven." (Matthew 16:19)

"And these attesting signs will accompany those who believe; in my name, they will cast out demons; they will speak with new tongues; they will take up serpents and if they drink

anything deadly, it will by no means hurt them; they will lay hands on the sick, and they will recover." (Mark 16:17).

"Behold, I have given you the authority to trample on serpents and scorpions, and over all the power of the enemy, and nothing shall by any means hurt you." (Luke 10:19)

Then something came to me by the Holy Spirit. He said, "You're missing the most important ingredient of all. Everything works by love." Wow! It hit me like a ton of bricks. I had perfected a lot of things, but the most important gift of all was missing—love! I saw some things happen in my ministry, but it does not compare with what is happening now. The thing that changed my life and ministry is my love walk. Please read the rest of this chapter and receive the words into your mind and heart. I believe that you will go to a new level in every area of your life. I believe your marriage and family will come closer together than you have ever been. If you have a wayward child, I believe he or she will be drawn back home. If you are separated from your spouse, I believe the rest of this chapter will bring restoration.

I Corinthians 13:13 says, *And now abide faith, hope, love, these three; but the greatest of these is love.* Everything in your Christian walk works by love. In the Amplified Bible, it says without love you are a useless nobody. Wow! This is where the rubber meets the road. Love never fails. We are talking about the "agape" unconditional love of God; a love that always believes the best of every person; a love that sees who people can become with the help of God. God is love and love never quits. It is always right there doing its job. Love knows that if it refuses to quit, it will ultimately win the victory. Lord, let us not lose heart and grow weary and faint in acting nobly and doing right, for in due time and at the appointed season we shall reap, if we do not loosen and relax our courage and faint (Galatians 6:9 AMP).

The scripture at the beginning of this chapter describes the unconditional love of God for us. He wants us to take the love He has for us and love others as He loves us.

Loving people unconditionally is a very big challenge. I would be tempted to say it is impossible, but since God tells us to do it, surely He must have a way for us to do it. He never commands us to do something and then leaves us to perform it on our own. His grace (His power, ability, and favor) is sufficient for us (2 Corinthians 12:9), meaning that He enables us to do what He has called us to do.

Sometimes we pray to be able to love the unlovely, and then do our best to avoid every unlovely person God sends our way. Some people are sent into our lives for the sole purpose of being sandpaper to us. We all have rough edges that need some sanding off at times. Learning to walk in love with unlovely people and learning to be patient in trials are probably the two most important tools God uses to develop our spiritual maturity. This is true in my life. Believe it or not, all those rude and obnoxious people in our lives help us. They sharpen and refine us for God's use.

He does not look for people who are worthy of His love. His love is unconditional. He looks for people who are in need of His love. That's why He chose me—and you. It was definitely the love of God that overcame evil in my life, that changed me and drew me into a deeper relationship with Him. It is that same love flowing through us to others that will change them. Most people who are difficult to love have suffered so much pain along the road of life that it has altered their personalities. Outwardly, they may seem hard and bitter, but inwardly they are crying out for love. That was the case for me. Outwardly I acted as if I needed no one, yet inwardly I was starving for love. Jesus said that He did not come for the well but for the sick (Matthew 9:12). Our world today is sick, from head to toe. The only answer for what ails us is Jesus Christ in all His Glory.

When you love your enemies, your enemies are defeated, even when they don't know it. When God's love shines through you, it changes the people around you, it changes the atmosphere, it changes the world. Ask God to change your heart toward your enemies. Ask Him to help you love them. You cannot do it by yourself. Only the transforming love of God can change you and your reactions to your enemies. Let Him do the work in you that needs to be done so He can use that transformation to defeat your enemies.

Prayer:

Lord Jesus, come into my heart and fill me with your love that never fails. Fill me with a love for my enemies that will defeat Satan. Thank you for life and life more abundantly. In Jesus' name, Amen.

Scripture to meditate on:

Behold, I have given you authority to trample on serpents and scorpions, and over all the power of the enemy and nothing shall by any means hurt you (Luke 10:19).

Chapter 9

Dreamers

Then they said to one another, "Look, this dreamer is coming!" (Genesis 37:19).

Joseph was a dreamer and he became the Prime Minister of an entire nation. He had to go through heartache after heartache to get there, but by the grace and power of God, he made it. There is so much to learn from Joseph's life recorded in the book of Genesis.

First, I want to encourage you to use wisdom in whom you tell your dreams to. Believe it or not, just because you are excited does not mean others will be too! As a matter of fact, most will hate you, just like Joseph's brothers hated him. I do not share my dreams and God-given visions with anyone anymore. They are between God and me alone. I learned this lesson the hard way. Just a few years ago I had everyone in my ministry turn their backs on me, except for one friend. Most people will become envious and jealous when God uses you in a great way, or out of wrong motives they will want to ride your coattail.

Thank God He gives us the gift of discernment. I only have three people around me that I trust, but I know that can change at any moment. All you have to do is look at how Peter denied Jesus. It can happen to anyone. That is why you must put all your trust in Jesus Christ alone. He is a friend that sticks closer than a brother. He will never leave you nor forsake you. He is with you always. You may not feel like it at times, but thank God we don't live by feelings, but we live by faith in the Son of God.

It is time to live as dreamers. I am speaking that over every person that reads this book. You are a dreamer! I believe God is about to give you dreams in a way that will astonish you. Get ready to be woken up in the middle of the night. You may wake up with an angel sitting on the end of your bed. He may give you a dream that seems absolutely impossible or inconceivable. Hear me clearly: when you hear something told to you that is impossible for you to do in the natural, then there is a very good chance that it is the voice of the Lord.

He will tell you to do things that you can not do apart from Him. You do what you can do in the natural and He will do what you cannot do. In other words, He puts His super on your natural, which makes it supernatural!

Stop limiting God!

Believe that entire cities can be won to Christ. Listen, when Jonah finally made it to Nineveh, the whole city was born again. God wants to do the same thing today.

I am asking God to give me the nations for His inheritance. I am believing and trusting God for things so big that as I said earlier in this chapter, I cannot tell anyone. They would think I was being prideful, or they would become jealous like Joseph's brothers.

Friends, there are dream-killers everywhere. The sad thing is most of them will never do anything to make a difference in our world today. More than that, they become enraged when they see someone who has a past like mine being used by God. Many wanted and still want to stone me. Just like the woman caught in adultery. They all wanted to stone her, until Jesus showed up and wrote in the sand. You who are without sin, cast the first stone. They all went away one by one.

See, we have all sinned and fallen short of the glory of God. Our righteousness is as filthy rags. Jesus told the woman, now go and sin no more. Those are the very words He spoke to me. See, I was the chiefest of all sinners, just like Paul, but God saved me out of a life of destruction, cleaned me up by washing me in the blood of Jesus, loved me until I loved myself, then He imparted a love in me, so I could love Him back with all my heart, soul, mind and strength, then finally taught me to love my neighbor as I love myself.

All of these things happened because I began to dream dreams that made no sense in the flesh. God talks crazy talk a lot of times, because His thoughts are higher than our thoughts, and His ways are higher than our ways. You have to pray and read the Bible. He says that you will know His voice, and the voice of a stranger you will not follow. God will never tell you to do something contrary to the Word of God. That is why you must read and study the Word of God. The Bible says, in the beginning was the Word, and the Word was with God and the Word was God. If you want to know Jesus, then read the Word. The Word became flesh. Jesus is the Word made flesh.

He came and dwelt among us and became our example. He was tempted and experienced everything we ever will go through, yet He was sinless. That is why the Bible says, come boldly to the throne of grace, so you can obtain mercy and grace in your time of need. He knows the answer to your every question. He has a way out of every trial you go through. He knows who your husband or wife is supposed to be. He wants to order your every step, because the steps of a good man are ordered by the Lord. If people would just wait on God, there would not be the divorce rate we are seeing, nor all the women being mentally, emotionally and physically abused like we are seeing in the world today.

My prayer is that you will begin to dream again. Believe in the impossible. See yourself as a world shaker and mover for

Jesus Christ. See yourself standing before many sharing your testimony and impacting your generation for Christ. See yourself as a Godly husband or wife. See your children being trained up in the ways of the Lord. See yourself healthy and whole. See yourself no longer smoking, drinking, drugging or being prideful. See yourself reduced to love. See yourself loving God with all your heart, soul, mind, and strength.

It all starts by dreaming and seeing you and others for who they can become through Christ. Everyone is worth loving and taking a chance on. God has made everyone in His image. Everyone has a soul, and God wants them saved, healed, and delivered. Time to dream dreamer!

Prayer:

Dear Jesus, I want to be a dreamer. I want to have faith in the impossible. Take my life and use it to bring You glory. In Jesus name I pray. Amen.

Scripture to meditate on:

I can do all things through Christ who strengthens me (Philippians 4:13).

Chapter 10

The Kingdom of Heaven

And from the days of John the Baptist until now the Kingdom of heaven suffers violence, and the violent take it by force (Matthew 11:12).

It is time to take back what the devil has stolen. I am tired of seeing the kingdom of heaven suffering violence, while people continue to die in their sin and populate hell.

The Bible says to be angry, but do not sin. I hate the devil and what he stands for. I hate and despise sin, not the sinner. I love the sinners and am determined to win them to Christ. Whatever it takes; whatever God wants to do in me and through me I will allow. To live is Christ and to die is gain. I have been bought by the blood of Jesus. I surrender all to Him. I count it an honor to suffer for my Lord and Savior.

Daily I present my body a living sacrifice to Him—holy and acceptable, which is my reasonable service. By the grace of God I will not be conformed by the renewing of my mind, so I can prove what is that good, acceptable, and perfect will of God.

I am proud to be a bondservant of my Lord and Savior. He is looking for a few good men and women. Will you answer the call? Will you hate Satan and what he is doing to people and families today? Understand friends, you must come to a place that you're not willing that anyone should perish. Cry out to God right now, and ask Him to give you a real burden and love for lost and hurting people. Hear me, people are dying every day and going into the lake of fire. Hell is consumed with people that denied and rejected Jesus Christ. God loves everyone, but He is holy and just. He gives everyone a chance. We must let God reduce us to love and impart mercy for the sinner into our hearts.

Today, I can truly say that I love everybody. It does not matter who it is. It can be the most evil and wicked person, yet I have a love and burden for that person. We do not wrestle against flesh and blood, but against principalities and powers of darkness. That is why we must love every sinner yet hate sin and the devil.

I am bent on populating heaven and advancing the Kingdom of God.

I know that God is going to restore everything that the devil stole from me, because He says so. He did it for Job and He will do it for Clark. In the meantime, I strive to win thousands to Christ through my Cross Times Radio program, as well as my books, YouTube, Facebook, and everywhere else that the Lord leads me.

As I said earlier in the book, the Lord desires to bring heaven to earth. He wants to unleash His Spirit through men, women and children in a way that shocks the world. The Third Great Awakening is right around the corner. The Lord is putting all pieces of the puzzle in place.

He is placing His ambassadors and warriors strategically in the four corners of the world. I don't know the day or time, but I know it is sooner than you think. Intercessors and prayer warriors have been warring in the Spirit realm for years now. Finally, they are about to experience the fruit of their labor. These warriors have been praying and fasting for this soon coming spiritual awakening. Revival fires are burning, the violent are ready to take back the Kingdom of heaven here on earth.

Listen, the same way God opened Elisha's servant's eyes, He wants to open your eyes. Hear me, there are more for us than there are against us. Listen to this scripture: *"Do not fear, for those who are with us are more than those who are with them." And Elisha prayed and said, "Lord, I pray, open his eyes that he may see." Then the Lord opened the eyes of the young man, and he saw. And behold, the mountain was full of horses and chariots of fire all around Elisha. So when the Syrians came down to him, Elisha prayed to the Lord, and said, "Strike this people, I pray, with blindness." And He struck them with blindness according to the word of Elisha"* (2 Kings 6:16-18).

You do not have to ever fear. The battle is the Lord's. He will tell you what to do and when to do it. Ask Him right now to open your eyes, that you might see all the armies of God around you too!

Now, go take the Kingdom of heaven by force.

Prayer:

Dear Jesus, open my eyes that I might see what Elisha's servant saw. Give me that boldness and fire for lost souls. In Jesus name I pray. Amen.

Scripture to meditate on:

"No weapon formed against you shall prosper, and every tongue that rises against you in judgment you shall condemn. This is the heritage of the servants of the Lord, and their righteousness is from me," says the Lord (Isaiah 54:17).

Chapter 11

The Prize

Not that I have already attained, or am already perfected; but I press on, that I may lay hold of that for which Christ Jesus has also laid hold of me. Brethren, I do not count myself to have apprehended; but one thing I do, forgetting those things which are behind and reaching forward to those things which are ahead. I press toward the goal for the prize of the upward call of God in Christ Jesus (Philippians 3:12-14).

If you are going to be unleashed into your world for the glory of God, then you have to press towards the prize. You have to let go of the past and the baggage it brings.

God is wanting to do a new thing in the world today. Old things have passed away and all things have become new. You know, I like to read about the great revivalists and men that God used for the other spiritual awakenings, but God does not want us to base this Third Great Awakening on the past revivals. Yes, I study those men God used. I want to know what they did in those times. They were sold out for Jesus. They did not play games with God. They certainly did not keep God in a box like so many do today. They lived a life of prayer and fasting. They spent most of their time alone with God. They were fearless and great men of faith. They preached the uncompromised Word of God. They were God-pleasers and not man-pleasers. They ticked off a lot of people. They were hated and lied about, just as Jesus was.

They preached with boldness as well as tears. They were humble and broken men. They knew that their strength came from their weakness. Pride had been crucified in them. They preached that there is a hell, and that apart from a relationship with Jesus Christ, that is where you go. They were not ashamed of the gospel. They knew that the gospel is the power of God unto salvation, to those who believe.

How many men and women of God does that describe today? Not many! I only know of a handful. Most preach a watered down gospel, tickling the ears of the hearers. Deceiving God's elect, due to the love of money and fame. God help us all! The prize I am talking about is the reward of salvation.

The Bible says, what does it profit a man to gain the whole world, yet lose his soul? I know many rich and materialistic people that are going straight to hell if they don't have an encounter with Jesus Christ the same way Paul did on the road to Damascus. It is going to take a bright light to blind them and knock them to the ground to get their attention. It's the same way with all those people having sex outside of marriage and living together outside of marriage. I have heard people say "I stay at her house, but we don't sleep together." They even tell me they sleep in the same bed. What an abomination to God. Let me tell you, if Jesus comes back and you're in that situation, hell has your number. The Bible says that it is better to have a millstone tied around your neck, and cast into the sea, then to be a stumbling block to someone.

If you are spending the night at someone's house outside of marriage, and the neighbor or a child knows you're there, you are a stumbling block. The Bible says to shun or avoid the appearance of evil. This is not to condemn you, but to open your eyes and allow God to lovingly convict you. Conviction will always draw you to Christ. Condemnation will turn you away from Him.

Sin gets your eyes off the prize. It blinds you. You have work to do for Christ. He is counting on you to live a holy life. He wants to use you to unleash His life into you, so you can point people in the direction of the prize. I want to encourage you right now to ask God to search your heart and expose to you the things that are leading you away from the prize. If you are not moving ahead with God, then you are going backwards. It is like riding a bike up a hill. If you are not pedaling upward, then you will fall backwards.

Forget the past. Old things are passed away and you cannot do anything about it. But you can certainly do something about your future. Today can be the first day of the rest of your life.

You may be thinking that your life has been falling apart, but I am here to tell you that your life is falling right into place. When you're down to nothing, God is up to something. He has chosen to use this book to get you focused on the prize he is talking about in the opening scriptures of this chapter. Go back and read it after we pray in a moment. Remember, let the past go. Look ahead and press toward the goal for the prize of the upward call of God in Christ Jesus.

Your greatest days are ahead. Now pray this prayer and allow God to unleash you to your generation for His glory.

Prayer:

Dear Jesus, come into my heart. I repent of my sin. Wash me in the blood of Jesus. Help me heal from the past hurts. Write my name in heaven. Now unleash your Spirit and your power into me so I can lead others to the prize. In Jesus name I pray. Amen.

Scripture to meditate on:

Draw near to God and He will draw near to you (James 4:8).

Chapter 12

An Awakening

And do this, knowing the time, that now it is high time to awake out of sleep; for now our salvation is nearer than when we first believed (Romans 3:16).

It is time to come to our senses, before it is too late.

America is in desperate need of an awakening from its sleep. It is so evident that pride and the love of money have gripped Americans today. Seems like it is all about the money, bigger houses, nicer cars, who can sleep with the most people, who can drink the most, do the most drugs, get the biggest from pumping iron, the tannest or the fittest. Flesh, flesh, and more flesh. The Spiritual Awakening that is about to hit Americans is going to shake the very core of these men and women. When God's holiness makes its way down, flesh will be consumed. People will die right in the middle of their sin. Read about Sodom and Gomorrah, or Ananias and Sapphire, or Lot's wife.

Friends, your warning is coming through the pages of this book. Do not be caught in adultery or sexual immorality in these last days.

God is an all consuming fire. He seeks purity and righteousness. The day is fast approaching that judgment is coming to the house of God as well as your own home. If you have pornography on your computer, or playboy books hidden in your home, you are going to be exposed. Get rid of it. Come out of darkness before God's bright light shines on you. America is about to experience a fear of God that will bring you to your knees. You have a chance to humble yourself right now so you don't have to be humbled publicly.

Open your eyes and ears. Hear what the Spirit of God is speaking to you off these pages. Let the peace of God rule in your hearts. Let your heart not be troubled. Pray, *search me O God and know my heart, try me and know my thoughts, see if there be any wicked way in me and lead me in the way everlasting* (Psalm 139:23-24).

You don't think it can get worse, but everything in America is about to be shaken, until there is nothing left that can be shaken. In these last days, if you are not in a relationship with Jesus Christ, with Him guiding you and protecting you, then fear is going to swallow you up. You must have God's protection or you have no protection at all. You are open game for Satan and his demons to steal, kill, and destroy you.

It is time to totally surrender your life to Jesus. He will unleash healing into your heart and mind. He will give you supernatural strength when you are weak. He will give you wisdom to know what to do at every turn in life. He will protect you and your family. He will provide for you when others are starving and crying out for help.

Believe in miracles. Believe that with God all things are possible. Believe that He will not allow any evil to touch you or your children. Trust in Him with all your heart, and don't lean to your own understanding. Put on the mind of Christ. It is more critical now than ever before. His thoughts are higher than your thoughts and His ways are higher than your ways.

Repent of any sin. Come to the cross and die to self. Take up your cross daily and follow Him. He has a great plan for your life. He is going to give you new dreams and visions. He is going to put the right people around you. He will remove stumbling blocks out of your way. He is going to take you into His secret place. You are the apple of His eye. He holds you in the palm of His hand. He is pouring out His Spirit on you right now. He is unleashing His perfect love into you right now, because perfect love casts out all fear. Fear is leaving you and faith is taking over.

Without faith it is impossible to please Him. Faith without works is dead. You walk by faith and not by sight. Speak things into existence. There is life and death in the power of the tongue. You will have what you speak. Speak life. Speak your future into existence. Call things that be not as though they are.

You are the head and not the tail. You are blessed and prosperous. You can do all things through Christ Jesus who strengthens you. You are blessed going out and blessed coming in. Everything you put your hands to prospers. Glory to God! I sense a spiritual awakening taking place in every reader's heart at this point of the book.

The Kingdom of God does not come with observation. You don't have to look to the right or to the left, but the Kingdom of God is within you. I don't know about you, but I am having revival in my heart, and that is why revival breaks out wherever I go.

It is so awesome when God unleashes Himself through you to lost, lonely, and hurting people. Get ready, I hear the wind blowing and the fire burning. Angels are on standby, ministries are preparing their churches, for multitudes are about to start running to the houses of God.

The Third Great Awakening is about to be unleashed into our world.

This is not a man's opinion, but God's Spirit saying "prepare ye the way of the Lord."

Prayer:

Dear Jesus, awaken me from my sleep and slumber. I repent of my sins and I ask you to wash me in the blood. Thank you for a Godly fear, which leads men to repentance. I surrender my life to you in Jesus name. Amen.

Scripture to meditate on:

For the wages of sin is death, but the gift of God is eternal life in Christ Jesus our Lord (Romans 6:23).

Chapter 13

Draw Near to God

Therefore, submit to God. Resist the devil and he will flee from you. Draw near to God and He will draw near to you.
(James 4:7-8)

If you will draw near to God, He will come running to meet you halfway. When you read the story of the Prodigal Son you realize that God is sitting there waiting for you to come home. *I will arise and go to my Father, and will say to him, "Father, I have sinned against heaven and before you, and I am no longer worthy to be called your son. Make me like one of your hired servants." And he arose and came to his father. But when he was still a great way off, his father saw him and had compassion and ran and fell on his neck and kissed him. And the son said to him, "Father, I have sinned against heaven and in your sight, and am no longer worthy to be called your son." But the father said to his servants, 'bring out the best robe and put it on him and put a ring on his hand and sandals on his feet. And bring the fatted calf here and kill it, and let us eat and be merry, for this my son was dead and is alive again; he was lost and is found. And they began to be merry."* (Luke 15:18)

Many of you reading this book should be jumping up and down praising God right now. You and I were like this Prodigal Son or daughter. We once were lost, but now we're found; were blind, but now we see. Glory to God! Others of you reading this book right now should repent of your sins and say this prayer:

Dear Jesus I ask you to forgive me of all my sins right now. I come home to you right now. I am so sorry for being one of those that has wasted my life to this point. Fill me with your spirit so I can serve you the rest of my days. In Jesus' name, I pray. Amen!

If you just prayed that prayer, then you can rest assured that God is right there with you to give you the best He has. Let Him love you and kiss you right now in Jesus' name. Praise Him. Tell Him how much you love Him and how grateful you are that He saved you from the pit of Hell. Your name is now written in the Lamb's Book of Life. He is going to restore to you all the years the devil stole from you. Glory to God!

The Prodigal Son is one of my favorite stories in the Bible, because God met me in my darkest moments and saved my soul, delivered me from hell, and has given me a life that is truly beyond what I ever dreamed possible. He has given me the best ring, robe, and fatted calf, too! Just like the Prodigal Son.

What is so amazing is that I did not have to earn or work for it. All I had to do was call upon the name of Jesus in my hurt and pain. He came running to comfort and hold me. It is because of His grace (unmerited favor) that I have a new life in and through Jesus Christ. He loved me so much that He took my sin and placed it at Calvary on that old rugged Cross. He shed His blood for the remission of my sins. On the third day, He arose from the dead and defeated death, hell, and the grave. He is seated at the right hand of the Father right now making intercession for you and me. This very moment Jesus is thinking about you as you read this book. Tell Him you love Him and need Him more than anything else. God inhabits the praises of His people.

The Lord drew near to me every time I drew near to Him. Whether it was in prison, jail, rehab, overdosing on drugs, about to drown at Lake Lavon, when I was about to hang myself in the cell in Houston, TX, or when I tried to commit suicide by slitting my wrist hoping to bleed to death. When God has called you, there is no devil in hell that can take you out. Just submit to God, resist the devil, and he will flee from you every time. God has a plan and purpose for your life or you would not be reading this book. By reading this book, you will have the courage and strength to serve God and cast out devils. Say, "Get thee behind me Satan, for it is written that you shall worship the Lord thy God, and Him only shall you serve." Let God arise and His enemies be scattered. When the enemy comes in like a flood, the Lord will raise up a standard against him every time. All you have to do is draw near to Him. He will do the rest.

Prayer:

Dear Jesus, I draw near to you. Your Word says that if I will draw near to You, then You will draw near to me. I submit to you, Lord, I resist the devil and now he flees in Jesus' name! Anoint me to always live for You in Jesus' name. Amen!

Scripture to meditate on:

Let us therefore come boldly to the throne of grace, that we may obtain mercy and find grace to help in time of need (Hebrews 4:16).

Chapter 14

Last Day Anointing

But you have an anointing from the Holy One and you know all things (1 John 2:20).

In these last days, it will take the anointing of the Holy One to save, heal, and deliver the human race.

God is unleashing His anointing through holy and righteous men, women, and children.

The anointing destroys the yokes of bondage. The anointing goes places in the body that no medicine can go, because Jesus is the Anointed One.

The anointing is the power source of the Holy Spirit.

Listen to this scripture: *"The Spirit of the Lord God is upon me, because the Lord has anointed me to preach good tidings to the poor; He has sent me to heal the brokenhearted, to proclaim liberty to the captives, and the opening of the prison to those who are bound; to proclaim the acceptable year of the Lord, and the day of vengeance of our God; to comfort all who mourn, to console those who mourn in Zion, to give him beauty for ashes, the oil of joy for mourning, the garment of praise for the spirit of heaviness; that they may be called trees of righteousness, the planting of the Lord, that He may be glorified,"* (Isaiah 61:1-3).

The anointing is powerful. The anointing can break the hardest heart. The anointing can convict and set free murderers, rapists, child molesters, alcoholics, drug addicts, whore mongers, prostitutes, those bound by pornography, as well as haters, backbiters, gossipers and thieves. Whatever you need deliverance from today, the Anointed One, Jesus Christ, is your answer.

With Him, all things are possible. No one is beyond help. Listen, Paul, once known as Saul, was a very wicked and cruel man. He murdered Christians, yet God said enough is enough, so He blinded him on the road to Damascus. The power of God knocked him and the others with him to the ground. This was the anointing. As you probably know, Paul wrote three-fourths of the New Testament and is still impacting the world for Jesus Christ. If the anointing could set him free and on fire for Jesus, then the anointing can set anybody free.

The last day anointing that is about to be poured out in the world will bring about miracles, signs and wonders beyond all human reasoning. I believe we will see more people raised from the dead than ever before. I believe we will see the lame walk, the blind see, and the deaf hear in supernatural ways. People that have been in wheelchairs for years will jump up, praise God and shout hallelujah all around the world. I believe many liquor stores will shut down from Holy Spirit conviction. I believe the pornographic industry will begin to go bankrupt in the last days, due to the anointing convicting them of their grave sin.

I believe that in churches around the world there will be people running to the altar crying out, "God, have mercy on me a sinner." This will happen without a preacher having to announce an altar call. All of this because of the anointing convicting people of sin, righteousness and judgment.

People you never thought would be saved or delivered will be the first in line. See, those who are bound by drugs, alcohol, pornography, etc. really don't want to do what they are doing. As I have always preached, hurting people hurt people. They only do what was done to them, or seen their parents or others do. They hate what they are doing in most cases. Homeless people don't want to live on the streets and eat out of trash cans. Prostitutes don't want to sell their bodies and risk their lives daily. They have been blinded, hurt, and have given themselves over to Satan.

But, this last day anointing is going to change all that mess.

The unleashing of the Third Great Awakening is going to blow your mind.

More than anything though, we will see hearts transformed, which will cause people to be saved or born again, whichever phrase you like. See, the greatest miracle is a life changed. Someone saved or born again, so they end up in heaven.

Listen to this scripture: *"Nevertheless do not rejoice in this, that the spirits are subject to you, but rather rejoice because your names are written in heaven,"* (Luke 10:20).

Make sure today that your name is written in heaven. Friends, if it is not, then you will end up in hell, separated from a loving God, where there are no more tears, sickness, disease, etc. Heaven will be beyond anything you or I can even begin to imagine in its beauty and wonder. But hell is filled with torment, burning, never sleeping, demons beating on you without ceasing, screaming, gnashing of teeth, where the worm never dies, etc. It is not a place you want to spend eternity. Hear me clearly, you will die one day, then there will be judgment. There is a heaven and a hell. The Bible makes it very clear, that few find heaven, and many find hell.

I want to encourage you today to choose life. When we get to the end of this chapter, make sure you are right with God. Pray the prayer and mean it to the best of your ability.

The anointing of God wants to fall fresh on you this day. God wants to write your name in the Lambs' Book of Life. You can make sure, in this moment of time, that you are heaven bound and not going to the Lake of Fire. You do not want to reject this offer my friend.

Here is your opportunity. Will you now set things right with Jesus Christ?

Prayer:

Dear Jesus, I repent of all my sins. I acknowledge that I am a sinner and in need of a Savior. Wash me in Your blood. Give me a new heart and life. I confess you as my Lord and Savior. I believe in my heart that God raised you from the dead. I believe my name is now written in heaven. Take my life and bring glory to You the rest of my days. In Jesus name I pray, Amen.

Scripture to meditate on:

That if you confess with your mouth the Lord Jesus and believe in your heart that God has raised Him from the dead, you will be saved. For with the heart one believes unto righteousness, and with the mouth confession is made unto salvation (Romans 10:9-10).

Chapter 15

My Cup Runs Over

You prepare a table before me in the presence of my enemies;You anoint my head with oil; my cup runs over. Surely goodness and mercy shall follow me all the days of my life; and I will dwell in the house of the Lord forever. (Psalm 23:5-6)

Over the years I have seen God show himself strong on my behalf when it comes to my enemies. I have always come out better in the long run. As a result of going to prison or jail, I can tell you that in those desperate times, I would always call out to the Lord. One of those times was on March 19, 1990, when I was "born again" in prison in Huntsville, TX. This was the place where it was just God and me. I had hit rock bottom in that prison cell. I felt like everybody had abandoned me, but God was right there as He always is. After I said the sinner's prayer, I can tell you that my cup ran over with the goodness of God. I had joy unspeakable and was full of glory. I was freer behind bars than most people are in the free world.

Thank God that He will make everything right at the appointed time (Habakkuk 2:3). Your enemies will be defeated before your face, the Lord says in Deuteronomy 28:7. They will come out against you one way and flee before you seven ways. It may look like they are winning at the moment, but believe me, if you will keep your heart pure and trust in the Lord with all your heart, God will show up and show out. He will bring the truth to light and there will be no denying that Jesus Christ is Lord, and you will be exalted above your enemies.

Those who have lied about you will be given over to a reprobate mind if they do not repent. The Lord will anoint your head with oil; your cup will run over if you stay faithful. He will never forsake the righteous. God is for you and not against you. He will right every wrong and expose every injustice done against you as long as you stay faithful.

Start loving your enemies, pray for them, and forgive them. Realize that God is working all your stuff together for good. His ways are higher than your ways and His thoughts are higher than your thoughts. God is so awesome. He never ceases to amaze me. God has a real sense of humor. All you have to do is look at Isaiah 54:11. *"Behold, I have created the blacksmith who blows the coals in the fire who brings forth an instrument for his work; and I have created the spoiler to destroy."*

Amazing how God even uses the devil to perfect His divine destiny for our lives. Thank God for the hard times. Thank God that He is sovereign and omnipresent. He is everywhere at all times. He knows that it is through the hard times that we, as humans, call out to Him. Sad that it has to come to that, but praise God He does not allow more on us than what we can handle. God is always refining us, purging us, stretching us, so that we can go to the next level.

Stop fighting against God and start working with Him. All you are going through is a test, either you pass it and get promoted, or you have to go back around the mountain and take the test again. Thank God that I have entered the promised land. It may have taken me 40 years—just like the Israelites—but I made it just in time to write this book. So, you can learn from my many failures in life. My pain, suffering, and trials were to teach you, so hopefully, you will listen and learn, so you can get promoted with less suffering. It is amazing the compassion God has put in my heart for my enemies. I pray daily for each of them. I truly love them and want them free from the bondage they are in. They are hurt, bitter, wounded people that need to have an encounter with the only One who can set them free. His name is Jesus Christ, the Holy One of Israel.

He was wounded for our transgressions, He was bruised for our iniquities; the chastisement for our peace was upon Him, and by His stripes we are healed (Isaiah 53:5).

If you are hurting, wounded, or just bitter because someone has hurt you, abused you, lied about you, left you for whatever reason, please pray this prayer. The Lord wants you to be healed and whole. He wants to give you a new life. With God all things are possible and nothing shall be impossible. I am living proof.

Prayer:

Lord Jesus, I repent of my sins. I repent of anger, hate, rebellion, unforgiveness, abusing others, gossiping and sowing discord. I ask you to wash me in the precious blood of Jesus. Please come into my heart and live in me by your Spirit. I will serve you the rest of my life as you empower me now in Jesus' name. Amen!

You are now free to move on and be all God has called you to be. Your dreams, visions, and desires are now coming to light. Glory to God!

Scripture to meditate on:

But my horn you have exalted like a wild ox; I have been anointed with fresh oil (Psalm 92:10).

Chapter 16

Pain at the Cross

He went a little further and fell on his face, and prayed, saying, "O my Father, if it is possible, let this cup pass from Me; nevertheless, not as I will, but as you will (Matthew 26:39).

Here is proof that Jesus Christ came down from heaven in the form of flesh. He was touched and tempted in every way that we are, yet without sin. Thank God for Jesus and His faithfulness to the Father.

Jesus suffered horribly and was rejected and hated just like many of us are today. When you take a stand for Christ, the world will do unto you what was done unto Jesus. John 15:20 says, *Remember the word that I said to you, "A servant is not greater than his master." If they persecuted me, they will also persecute you. If they kept my word, they will keep yours also.*

For many years I knew Christ, but I was not willing to die for Him. I would give Him certain things in my life, but I had idols that kept me bound and separated from His presence and blessings. Sure, He protected me from death, just like He did Job; the enemy can only do what God permits him to do, nothing more. But the consequences were painful beyond words. It is one thing to suffer for doing right as I know today, but when you have to suffer for sin whether it be pride, drugs, alcohol, hate, unforgiveness, bitterness, and so forth it is not worth it.

Because of God's grace and mercy, I finally came out of the wilderness after 40-something years of hell on earth. But there are many that have died and gone to hell as a result of sin. Many could not bear the pain, so they blew their brains out or committed suicide in another way. Many have overdosed due to the pain, suffering, and depression caused by sin. The Bible says, *The wages of sin is death* (Romans 6:23). The Bible also says that if you sow to the flesh you will reap corruption (Galatians 6:8). Many are sick today as a result of sin. Many have lost their minds due to sin. The penalty is damnation, my friends, and the lake of fire (hell) awaits those who don't turn to Jesus Christ, repent, and make Him Lord and Savior of their lives.

I have such a burden to see people move out of darkness into His marvelous light. Friends, please listen to a man who went through things beyond description, but I am now alive, free, on fire for the Lord, in love with Jesus, and in love with people because of His grace and mercy only. No peace or joy exists apart from Jesus Christ being Lord of your life.

He is calling out your name today to the Father. He loves you so much. He wants to give you a new life of love, peace, joy, goodness, kindness, patience, and so much more. He wants you to be happy and blessed. Ask Jesus to help you, and He will come running. If you are reading this book today, then you need to know that God has not given up on you. The devil could have killed you if not for God having His hand on your life. You are in the right place at the right time, my friend.

God has a plan and purpose for your life, and it starts today. Romans 8:28 says, *"And we know that all things work together for good for those who love God, to those who are the called according to his purpose."*

Satan has tried to kill you and me time after time. The so-called religious crowds have rejected you and me and ridiculed us. At times even those that have supported us have left us abused and forsaken. But God will never allow us to be confounded before men. He will never allow us to be dismayed or put to shame before the world. What a mighty God we serve. To God be the glory for all He has done and is continuing to do in you and me.

Prayer:

Dear Jesus, no longer will I push away the cup of suffering. With you, all things are possible. Give me Your power in place of my weakness and be glorified in all I do. Amen.

Scriptures to Meditate On

My Brethren, count it all joy when you fall into various trials, knowing that the testing of your faith produces patience. But let patience have its perfect work, that you may be perfect and complete lacking nothing (James 1:2-4).

Chapter 17

The Blood Spill

But if we walk in the light as He is in the light, we have fellowship with one another, and the blood of Jesus Christ His Son cleanses us from all sin (1 John 1:7).

What can wash away my sin? Nothing but the blood of Jesus. What can make me whole again? Nothing but the blood of Jesus. Revelation 12:11 says, and they overcame him by the blood of the Lamb and by the word of their testimony, and they did not love their lives to the death.

Friends, there never would have been the remission of sins without the shedding of the blood of Jesus Christ at the cross. How could we not give our lives to Christ after what He did for us at the cross?

My prayer is that this book will bring you to your knees, and that you go back to the cross and die to everything that is keeping you from surrendering all to Jesus. It could be sports, drugs, alcohol, gambling, a girlfriend or boyfriend, hate, unforgiveness, bitterness, or could even be your wife, husband, or children. Whatever you are putting before the Lord in your life needs to be put at the foot of the cross. You need to repent and let the precious blood of the Lamb wash you white as snow.

God will give you the desires of your heart, as long as you put Him first. Give Him your mates and children, and He will come and make your family exceedingly abundantly above all that you can ever ask or think (Ephesians 3:20). That is great news. Many of you reading this book need a miracle. You need to go back to the cross and repent of all your sins. You need to return to your first love, Jesus Christ. You need the resurrection power of Jesus Christ to raise you from the dead once you die. Then you can say what Paul said in 1 Corinthians 2:2: *For I determined not to know anything among you except Jesus Christ and Him crucified.* Then you can stand on Philippians 3:10 where Paul said, *"That I may know Him and the power of His resurrection."*

Friends, the reason I am writing this book is because I lived through and had to suffer horrible consequences for not obeying what I am writing to you about. These truths come from real life experiences. But by the grace of God, I went to the cross and finally died to Clark so that the Lord by His Spirit could resurrect the very life of Jesus in me. Today I am crucified with Christ, nevertheless I live, yet not I but Christ in me. I am now an overcomer by the blood of the Lamb, and I am now qualified to write this book, so you too will overcome and be all God has called you to be. Remember, it all starts at the cross and it all ends at the cross.

Repent of your sins. Ask God to forgive you, and mean what you say. Let the tears flow and brokenness and humility come. Tears are healing. Let God do the surgery in your heart that needs to be done. Stop letting the devil lie to you. You're more than a conqueror. Greater is He who is in you than he that is in the world. You can do all things through Christ Jesus who strengthens you.

The wages of sin is death, but the free gift of God is eternal life in Christ Jesus. God formed you in your mother's womb before you were ever born. (Jeremiah 1:5) He has a plan for you and there is nobody that can do it like you. Rise up, take your place in the army of the Lord. Fight the good fight of faith, and stop looking back. Press toward the mark for the prize of the high calling of God in Christ Jesus. This is a new day and a new beginning for you. A family that prays together stays together. So start praying and continually give God all the glory and thanks for what He has done, is doing, and will do until His Son Jesus returns on that white horse with fire in His eyes to take back what belongs to Him. Glory to God!

Prayer:

Dear Jesus, thank you for willfully dying for me. Thank you for shedding your blood to wash away all my sin. I am so sorry for putting you on that cross, but from this day forward I will take back what belongs to my soul. In Jesus name. Amen!

Scriptures to Meditate on:

In Him we have redemption through His blood, the forgiveness of sins according to the riches of His grace (Ephesians 1:7).

Chapter 18

Crucified With Christ

I have been crucified with Christ; it is no longer I who live, but Christ who lives in me; and the life which I now live in the flesh I live by faith in the Son of God, who loved me and gave Himself for me (Galatians 2:20).

This chapter contains the instructions to show you how to be unleashed.

You must die to self. You must be crucified with Christ. It is not enough just to go to the cross, but you must be broken and brought to the end of yourself. It can only happen when you surrender your life, dreams, visions, mate, children, cars, homes, and idols to Him, Jesus Christ, who bought you with His blood. This is the greatest demonstration of love that has ever been shown. Who for the joy that was set before Him (Jesus) endured the cross; despising the shame, and has sat down at the right hand of the throne of God.

Friends, let this day be the end of your life; that Christ may once and for all take over residence in your body. Can you speak 1 Corinthians 6:19 and mean it? Do you know that your body is the temple of the Holy Spirit who is in you, whom you have from God, and you are not your own? Your greatest days are ahead. This is the first day of the rest of your life. You will never be the same, and neither will your mate, nor your children, nor your church, nor your work place, nor your new business, nor your new ministry. Hallelujah! You have finally been crucified with Christ. Finally, you have not only gone to the cross, but you died! Glory to God!

You are now a light in every dark place. You are now reconciled everywhere you go. When you walk into a room, the whole atmosphere changes. When you walk into a room, I can hear people already saying, "That is a man of God," or "That is a woman of God." That hate you once had, say goodbye to it. That bitterness that was once rooted in you and defiled many, say goodbye to it. Now hear the words of your heavenly Father this minute:

"You are forgiven."

How about your best friend, fear? Well, he died at the cross with you. Say goodbye to fear once and for all.

Now, welcome your best friends into your new home. Meet love, joy, peace, patience, kindness, goodness, faithfulness, and self-control. They will never leave you nor forsake you as long as you deny yourself, take up your cross daily and follow Jesus. Remember, without faith it is impossible to please Him (Hebrews 11:6). Walk hand in hand with faith. The greatest gift of all is love, because faith and every other gift works by love. Without love you and I are nothing. And remember to love your enemies, bless those who curse you, do good to those who hate you, and pray for those who spitefully use you and persecute you (Matthew 5:44). This is only possible when you have gone to the cross and died once and for all. Isn't this the greatest love story of all?

This is almost like a fairy tale, but I know it to be true. You see, after many years of going to the cross, I finally not only went there, but by the grace of God, in a jail cell of all places, I finally surrendered my life to Jesus and died there. The benefits have been exceedingly, abundantly above anything I could have ever asked or thought (Ephesians 3:20). With men this is impossible, but with God all things are possible. You see, I lived that, too. Please hear my story and learn from it my friends. You see, I am like Paul and Joseph; I went to prison. Like Peter, too, denied Christ. Oh yes, David and I had a lot in common too, but thanks be to God, he says over me what he said over David, "Clark is a man after my own heart." I also am a little like Jeremiah. I can say, "The Word of God is like fire shut up in my bones." And well, Job and I had a lot in common. I, too, lost everything; yet by the grace of God, I have overcome and what I lost is on its way back as I write this book. The last chapter of my life story is yet to be written.

I tell you all these things that you might know that I have gone before you and paid the price, so that if you will hear the voice of the Lord off these pages, and heed His every instruction, you will not have to suffer all the hell I went through. Yes, there will still be suffering and pain, but you will have the strength and courage to overcome. You won't have to go to jail, prison, insane, hell, divorce court, AA, NA, anymore, just soak in the presence of God and let Him take you places you never dreamed of.

Dream dreamers, and believe in the impossible. Signs and wonders are now going to follow you everywhere you go. The blessings of God are running you down and overtaking you. You have gone to the cross and died. Now you shall live a life that pleases God and brings great glory to Jesus Christ. I love you and I am so proud of you.

Now it is time for you to be unleashed into your world to demonstrate the Spirit and power of God. You have gone to the cross and died to self. You are now useable for the Lord. Go and impact your world.

Prayer:

Dear heavenly Father, thank you that I am crucified with Your Son Jesus, yet I live to give You glory in all I do. Amen!

Scripture to meditate on:

Surely goodness and mercy shall follow me all the days of my life, and I will dwell in the house of the Lord forever (Psalm 23:6).

Chapter 19

Unleashed

For the vision is yet for the appointed time; But at the end it will speak, and it will not lie. Though it tarries, wait for it; Because it will surely come, it will not tarry (Habakkuk 2:3).

Here we are at the last chapter of another book; but this is not just another book. I hope and pray that you will heed the words of this book. May this book encourage you to be a big part of God Almighty unleashing His Spirit and power as He ushers in the Third Great Awakening. This Spiritual Awakening will be unleashed through faithful men and women who have sold out for Jesus Christ.

Begin to pray and fast as the Spirit of God leads you. Spend as much time in the Word of God and His presence as you possibly can. What is about to happen is well worth the sacrifice it costs you.

The Bible says to live is Christ, and to die is gain. I am so excited that this spiritual awakening is coming at God's appointed time. What an honor and blessing to live in this time. Many have had visions over the years, but now is the appointed time. Though it tarried for many years, it will surely come when many of you least expect it. I am only a man, but a man that hears from God. You want to prepare this day for what is about to be unleashed into our world here. God spoke it to me, and He will do what He has said He will do. Take heed or you will be swallowed up by the enemy and everything he stands for.

If you will believe by faith what you are hearing through this book, which I believe is inspired by God, you will be drawn into a secret place with the Lord, where He will confirm His Word and prepare your heart for this spiritual awakening.

Unleashed is a title the Lord gave me two years ago. As I told you at the beginning of this book, He stopped me in my tracks at a radio station before one of my Cross Times Radio programs. Now, I know why. He just showed me as I was penning the last sentence. Wow! Timing is everything with God. You must be in the right place at the right time, or, as the scriptures says at the beginning of this final chapter, at the appointed time. I feel His presence flowing out of my belly like rivers of living water. Heed these words my friends!

When I began to write *Unleashed* two years ago, it was not the right time. If I had not heard and obeyed His voice and wrote the book, then I would have been humiliated today, because the unleashing has not happened yet. But God had me write another book back then called *Thank God For My Cross*. He wanted people saved though that book, so they would be ready for this new book. Thank you, Jesus, for this revelation!

Friends, NOW is the time! It is no accident you are reading and finishing this book today. The Lord will give people time to hear, then He will suddenly appear by fire. His glory will fill the earth. People will begin to fall on their knees in grocery stores as they walk by you in the aisles. People will fall out under the power of God in parking lots of churches around the world. As I said before, liquor stores, pornographic shops, and other grotesque places of business will shut down from a fear of God! People will begin to see hell and themselves falling into the lake of fire while hearing the uncompromised Word of God preached. They will run to the altars repenting and crying out to a Holy God, as they begin to see Him as He really is.

Many people will begin to have visits from angels.

As all these great things are happening, remember this, the devil and all his demons will be bringing many under deception, where many people will believe his lies. There will also be a great falling away. Many will rise up against you and me. Many will be martyred for preaching the blood, the cross, and the resurrection of Jesus Christ. It happened in the days of old, and it will happen in the upcoming days. Pray without ceasing. Be alert and stay sober. Run from sin and anything that looks like it. Abstain from the very appearance of evil.

Listen to this scripture: *For the eyes of the Lord run to and fro throughout the whole earth, to show Himself strong on behalf of those whose heart is loyal to Him* (2 Chronicles 16:9).

God is your power source. He is your protector from all evil. He will deliver you out of all your troubles, if you will sell out to him. No compromise. Totally surrendered vessels, useful for the master, prepared for every good work.

We are in a war, but we have already won the battle. The end of the story has already been told from the beginning. Trust in the Lord with all your heart; lean not on your own understanding, and He will lead you into all truth.

Meditate on this next scripture, because times will get tough very soon. You will see evil all around you, but here is your promise: *A thousand may fall at your side, and ten thousand at your right hand; but it shall not come near you* (Psalm 91:7).

What a promise! I can tell you that through all the things I have gone through in my life, whether prison, jail, drug addiction, alcoholism, gambling addiction, heart attack, stroke, blind from a drug overdose, abuse, or suicide attempts, God has always been faithful. He has always delivered me and saved me out of all my troubles. He is a loving, merciful, gracious, and awesome God. He loves you so much that He sent His son, Jesus Christ to the world to be murdered for you and me. This is the only way that you and I could be saved from the penalty of death and then hell. We are all guilty, and apart from a relationship with Jesus Christ through his death, burial, and resurrection, we would all be there.

But thanks be to God, Jesus is alive and well today, praying for you and me at the right hand of the throne of God. I believe Jesus is saying something like this today: "Father, thank you for having mercy on all humanity today. Now is the appointed time to unleash heaven to earth. Let's send the Third Great Awakening, so we can win the world back to us. In the power of the name you have given me I pray this. Amen."

Prayer:

Dear Jesus, thank you for unleashing the Third Great Awakening to the world. We need you! In Jesus Name I pray, Amen.

Scripture to meditate on:

The Lord is not slack concerning His promise, as some count slackness, but is longsuffering toward us, not willing that any should perish, but that all should come to repentance (2 Peter 3:9).

Appendix

The Sinner's Prayer

The Bible says, *"God so loved the world that He gave his only Son, that whoever believes in Him shall not perish but have everlasting life"* (John 3:16). All of us have done, said, or thought things that are wrong. This is called sin.

Our sins have separated us from God. The Bible says, *"All have sinned and fall short of the glory of God"* (Romans 3:23). God is perfect and holy, and our sins separate us from God forever. The Bible says, *"The wages of sin is death, but the gift of God is eternal life through Jesus Christ our Lord"* (Romans 6:23).

God sent his only Son, Jesus Christ, to die for our sins. Jesus is the Son of God. He lived a sinless life and then died on the cross to pay the penalty for our sins. *"God demonstrates how his own love for us in that while were yet sinners Christ dies for us"* (Romans 5:8). Jesus rose from the dead and now He lives in Heaven with God His Father. He offers us the gift of eternal life—of living forever with Him in Heaven if we accept Him as our Lord and Savior. Jesus, said, *"I am the way and the truth and the life. No one comes to the Father accept by me"* (John 14:6).

God reaches out in love to you and wants you to be His child. *"As many as received Him, to them gave the right to become children of God, only to those who believe in His name"* (John 1:12).

You can choose to ask Jesus Christ to forgive you of your sins and come into your life as your Lord and Savior. If you want to accept Christ as your Savior and turn from your sins, you can ask Him to be your Savior by praying a prayer like this:

"**Lord Jesus, I believe you are the son of God. Thank You for dying on the cross for my sins. Please forgive my sins and give me the gift of eternal life. I ask You into my life and heart to be my Lord and Savior. I want to serve You always." Amen.**

Did you pray this prayer? If so, please contact me and I will be glad to assist you in your new walk with Jesus.

I WANT TO HEAR FROM YOU!

Beloved, if you have prayed that simple prayer, I believe you have been born again. Your name has been written in the Lamb's Book of Life in Heaven. You will spend eternity with God. This is the greatest decision you have ever made.

I encourage you to get involved in a Bible-based church and keep God in first place in your life.

I love you and will be praying for you.

I also would love to hear from you!

To contact me, write to:

Cross Times
P.O. Box 570131
Dallas, Texas 75357
214-306-3061
Email:clark@crosstimes.com
Website:www.crosstimes.com
www.facebook.com/crosstimesradio1

Enjoy Clark's other books

Thank God I Got Caught—From Prisoner to Worshiper:
Thank God I got caught with 10,000 hits of ecstasy and $40,000 cash on September 23, 1988. Clark Crawford was convicted of "conspiracy to possess a controlled substance" on January 12, 1990, and was given 20 years in the Texas Department of Corrections (Prison). Clark was devastated since the judge had told him that he would get 10 years "deferred adjudicated probation". All Clark could remember is his mother screaming out in the courtroom as the sentence was read and he was taken away.

Find out why 20 years later Clark wrote, *Thank God I Got Caught—From Prisoner To Worshipper.*

Thank God For My Enemies:
Clark Crawford has been reduced to love because of his enemies and has learned the real meaning of forgiveness because of some recent events by those whom he thought loved him. In Genesis 15:20, Joseph said to his brothers, who sold him into slavery, *"But as for you, you meant it for evil against me; but God meant it for good, in order to bring it about as it is on this day, to save many people alive."* Clark has learned firsthand, but I say to you, love your enemies, bless those who curse you, do good to those who hate you, and pray for those who spitefully use you and persecute you (Matthew 5:44). You will look at your enemies in a whole different light after reading this power packed book inspired by God.

Thank God for My Cross

Clark not only speaks with a biblical mandate, but also through years of experience. He knows what it feels like to be lost, and he knows what it feels like to be found in Christ. Clark also knows what a half-hearted commitment is like compared to selling out completely to Christ. Clark speaks with boldness, yet with compassion. He shows you the joy of following Jesus and victory in the Holy Spirit. You will also discover a soul-winner's heart and a man who has a burden for hurting humanity. Every chapter of this anointed book explains the step-by-step process to total victory over every bondage in your life. You will discover great teaching on the blood of Christ, sanctification and common sense Christianity.

All four of Clark's books, including *Unleashed*, are available by ordering on the internet at *www.crosshousebooks.com*, *www.amazon.com*, *www.barnesandnoble.com*, and at other on-line and physical bookstores as well as Clark's own website:

www.crosstimes.com

You can also contact Clark by phone and he will be glad to send you a copy.

How is God Unleashing His Power Through You?

Scripture says that we overcome the enemy by the blood of the lamb and the word of our testimony. Please use this page and the next one to write down a short testimony of the changes you've seen in your life from reading this book and how God is now unleashing His Spirit through you and then share it with others.

Now below make a list of all the areas in your life that you have not given over to God that He is not currently working through. Feel free to use the next blank pages as well. Find someone you can use as an accountability partner that you can share this with and have them pray with you.

1.

2.

3.

4.

5.

6.

7.

8.

9.

10.

www.ingramcontent.com/pod-product-compliance
Lightning Source LLC
Chambersburg PA
CBHW052107070526
44584CB00017B/2367